HOW CAN WE KNOW WE'LL GO TO HEAVEN?

RANDY ALCORN

HOW CAN WE KNOW WE'LL GO TO HEAVEN?

A recent poll indicated that for every American who believes he or she is going to hell, there are 120 who believe they're going to heaven.

This optimism stands in stark contrast to Jesus Christ's words written in the Bible: "Enter by the narrow gate. For the gate is wide and the way is easy that leads to destruction, and those who enter by it are many. For the gate is narrow and the way is hard that leads to life, and those who find it are few" (Matthew 7:13–14).

The truth is that according to the Bible we don't automatically go to heaven. In fact, hell—not heaven—is our default destination. Unless our sin problem is solved once and for all, we can't enter heaven. That's the bad news.

But once that's straight in our minds we're ready to hear the good news of Jesus Christ. Jesus took upon himself, on the cross, the hell we deserve so that we could experience for eternity the heaven we don't deserve!

The point of Romans 8:32 is that this love of God for his one and only Son was like a massive, Mount Everest obstacle standing between God and our salvation. Here was an obstacle almost insurmountable. Could God—would God—overcome his cherishing, admiring, treasuring, white-hot, infinite, affectionate bond with his Son and hand him over to be lied about and betrayed and denied and abandoned and mocked and flogged and beaten and spit on and nailed to a cross and pierced with a sword, like an animal being butchered and hung up on a rack?

The unthinkable reality that Romans 8:32 affirms is that God did it. He did hand him over. God did not spare him. In this passage Paul is saying the most unthinkable thing: God handed over his Son to death. "This Jesus [was] delivered up according to the definite plan and foreknowledge of

God" (Acts 2:23). God himself handed over his Son. Nothing greater or harder has ever happened. Or ever will.

> NOTHING, NOT ... OR FAMINE OR ... CAN SEPARATE ... OF GO[D]

Therefore, God has done the hardest thing to give us everlasting happiness. He did not spare his own Son but gave him up for us all. What does this guarantee? Paul puts it in the form of a rhetorical question (that means a question he expects us to immediately answer correctly): "how will he not also with him graciously give us all things?" "All things" is not a promise of a trouble-free life. Four verses later Paul says, "For your sake we are being killed all the day long; we are regarded as sheep to be slaughtered" (Rom. 8:36). Instead, "all other name under heaven given among men by which we must be saved" (Acts 4:12). Because of Jesus Christ's sacrificial death on the cross on our behalf, God freely offers us forgiveness.

To be forgiven, we must recognize and repent of our sins. Forgiveness is not automatic. It's conditioned upon confession: "If we confess our sins, he is faithful and just to forgive us our sins and to cleanse us from all unrighteousness" (1 John 1:9). Christ offers to everyone the gifts of forgiveness, salvation, and eternal life. "Let the one who is thirsty come; let the one who desires take the water of life without price" (Revelation 22:17).

There's no righteous deed we can do that will earn us a place in heaven (Titus 3:5). We come to Christ empty-handed. We can take no credit for salvation. "For by grace you have been saved through faith. And this is not your own doing; it is the gift of God, not a result of works, so that no one may boast" (Ephesians 2:8–9). This gift cannot be worked for, earned, or achieved. It's dependent solely on Christ's generous sacrifice on our behalf.

Now is the time to make things right with God. Confess your sinfulness and accept the sacrifice of Jesus Christ on your behalf.

You are made for a person and a place. Jesus is the person, and heaven is the place. They are a package—they come together. You cannot get heaven without Jesus or Jesus without heaven. "Seek the LORD while he may be found; call upon him while he is near" (Isaiah 55:6). For all eternity you'll be glad you did.

If you understand what God has done to make forgiveness and eternal life possible for you, you may want to express it in words like these: "Dear Lord, I confess that I do not measure up to your perfect standard. Thank you for sending Jesus to die for my sins. I now place my trust in him as my Savior. Thank you for your forgiveness and the gift of eternal life."

Bible references: ESV.

www.goodnewstracts.org